EYEWITNESS READERS

PROFICIENT
4
READERS

PIRATES!

RAIDERS OF THE HIGH SEAS

Written by Christopher Maynard

D1304918

DORLING KINDERSLEY

London • New York • Moscow • Sydney

Shoot, slash and steal!

Whenever law and order is weak and riches easy to come by, that's when pirates thrive the most. Those who get caught know the penalty is death. But the lonely high seas are an easy place for a pirate to hide.

Captain Kidd
(Gardiner's Island, 1699)
Captain Kidd stashed some of his treasure on this tiny island. The haul included sacks of gold dust, silver bars, and precious stones.
See page 30.

CANADA

NORTH AMERICA

Boston
New York

OAK ISLAND

GARDINER'S ISLAND

Virginia

North Carolina

South Carolina

ATLANTIC OCEAN

Caribbean

HISPANIOLA

JAMAICA

Portobelo
Panama City

SOUTH AMERICA

Blackbeard
(North Carolina, 1718)
This giant of a man was so mad and bad that he terrified his shipmates almost as much as the unfortunate victims of his pirate raids.
See page 40.

Henry Morgan
(Panama City, 1671)
This brilliant buccaneer didn't chase after ships. His goal was to raid the richest Spanish town in Central America.
See page 22.

A Note to Parents and Teachers

Eyewitness Readers is a compelling new reading programme for children. *Eyewitness* has become the most trusted name in illustrated books and this new series combines the highly visual *Eyewitness* approach with engaging, easy-to-read stories. Each *Eyewitness Reader* is guaranteed to capture a child's interest while developing his or her reading skills, general knowledge and love of reading.

The books are written by leading children's authors and are designed in conjunction with literacy experts, including Cliff Moon M.Ed., Honorary Fellow of the University of Reading. Cliff Moon spent many years as a teacher and teacher educator specializing in reading. He has written more than 140 books for children and teachers and he reviews regularly for teachers' journals.

The four levels of *Eyewitness Readers* are aimed at different reading abilities, enabling you to choose the books that are exactly right for each child.

Level One – Beginning to read
Level Two – Beginning to read alone
Level Three – Reading alone
Level Four – Proficient readers

The "normal" age at which a child begins to read can be anywhere from three to eight years old, so these levels are intended only as a general guideline.

No matter which level you select, you can be sure that you're helping children learn to read, then read to learn!

A Dorling Kindersley Book
www.dk.com

Project Editor Penny Smith
Art Editors Andrew Burgess and
Susan Calver
Senior Editor Linda Esposito
Managing Art Editor Peter Bailey
Production Josie Alabaster
Picture Researcher Christine Rista
Illustrator Peter Dennis

Reading Consultant
Cliff Moon M.Ed.

Published in Great Britain by
Dorling Kindersley Limited
9 Henrietta Street
London WC2E 8PS

4 6 8 10 9 7 5

Visit us on the World Wide Web at http://www.dk.com

Eyewitness Readers™ is a trademark of
Dorling Kindersley Ltd.

A CIP catalogue record for this book is
available from the British Library.

ISBN 0-7513-5714-6

Colour reproduction by Colourscan
Printed and bound in Belguim by Proost

The publisher would like to thank the following
for their kind permission to reproduce their photographs:
c=centre; t=top; b=below; l=left; r=right

Bridgeman Art Library, London: Private Collection 7b, 46;
Victoria & Albert Museum, London: 6t; British Museum,
London: 7t, 9t, 10t, 10b, 12; Mary Evans Picture Library: 6b, 9b,
20, 22, 27t, 28, 33b, 36; Ronald Grant Archive: front jacket (l and
b inserts); Robert Harding Picture Library: 19b; Museum of
London: 27c, 35t, 40; National Maritime Museum, London: front
jacket t insert, 16, 18c, 18b, 18t, 19t, 23, 25t, 29, 30, 33t, 42b, 44t,
47; Public Record Office Picture Library: Crown copyright
material 31t; Rye Town Hall: 34; Telegraph Colour Library:
D Noton front jacket (background), White's Electronics 38

Contents

Shoot, slash and steal! 4

Kidnapped! 6

Filthy rich! 14

Wild buccaneers 22

Captain Kidd 30

Treasure Island 38

Mad, bad Blackbeard 40

Glossary 48

Over the centuries just the sight of a pirate flag has been enough to strike terror into the hearts of sailors.

In this book are some of the most famous pirates of all. The map shows where they once roamed – and where they are lurking in the pages ahead.

Pirates of the Roman empire (Mediterranean Sea, 78 BC)
Julius Caesar is known as a great Roman leader. But his story could have turned out differently when he was kidnapped by pirates. See page 6.

IRELAND
ENGLAND
• Bristol
FRANCE
SPAIN
Rome •
GREECE
Mediterranean Sea
RHODES
Mecca •
SAUDI ARABIA
AFRICA
INDIAN OCEAN
ATLANTIC OCEAN
MADAGASCAR

Captain Avery (Indian Ocean, 1695)
Captain Avery and his motley crew got more than they bargained for when they pursued the treasure fleet of the richest man in India. See page 14.

Kidnapped!

Of all the masters in Rome, I end up serving the proudest of all. By the gods! He's enough to make a sweet-tempered slave like me want to curse!

My master is Julius Caesar, son of a noble family. Great things are expected of him. But why he wanted to go and study on the island of Rhodes, I have no idea.

"Pack for a long voyage, Didius," he commanded me one day. He knows full well that I get seasick, but he pays no heed.

When we boarded the slow sailing tub that was to take us to Rhodes, my heart sank. It was packed with wine and olive oil and reeked like a compost heap. To cap it all, the only room for me was on deck in the sun!

The first week was awful. We crawled along at a turtle's speed.

And the jars of wine kept falling over. They covered me with warm, sticky liquid. By the time we reached the coast of Greece I was sick *and* dirty.

Then just when I felt my luck couldn't get any worse, it did. That morning the captain went to Master Julius, looking very worried.

"There's a ship behind us and it's catching up fast," he said. "It's a small, rowing galley. In these waters it can only mean one thing – pirates!"

In next to no time the galley pulled alongside. The pirates gave us a choice. Drop sail and let them on board – or die! We dropped sail.

Storage jars
These clay vessels, called amphorae, were shaped so they could be tightly packed on merchant ships.

Rowing galleys
Oarsmen were usually slaves or prisoners. They sat below deck in horribly hot and smelly conditions.

The pirates swarmed aboard, waving swords and knives. They pushed us to the ground and tied our hands and feet. Then they loaded the wine and olive oil on to their ship. Next they dragged us to our feet and herded us back to their ship.

My master was not used to this kind of treatment.

"Do you know who I am?" he demanded angrily. "I am the noble Julius Caesar of Rome! Do you have any idea what will happen to you if you harm me?"

Sometimes, I fear, my master's temper gets the better of him.

"You'll regret it to your dying day!" he roared.

The villainous pirates burst out laughing. They were not afraid of Caesar.

The pirate leader waved his sword in Master Julius's face.

"Listen, you little toga! You're worth much more alive than dead. Every time you make a fuss your ransom doubles."

Caesar scowled furiously but did not speak. The pirate's sword was too near his neck.

The pirate sneered. "And there's always the slave market for you if your family refuses to pay. A young man ought to fetch a decent price. Though I don't suppose you know the meaning of the word *work*."

Ransom money
Kidnapping a rich noble and demanding cash for his return was an easy way to get money. Roman coins featured gods, leaders and major events.

Buying a slave
Children of other slaves were the most expensive. They knew how to work hard and take orders.

Writing tools
Romans wrote
with pens
dipped in ink.
The ink was
made from
sooty water.
Writers also
scratched letters
into wax tablets.

Roman rings
Wealthy nobles
wore gold rings
as a sign of
rank. They
used rings with
carved stones to
seal documents.

The pirates rowed us to a tiny island where they had a base. They lived in a few rundown houses, which were overlooked by a crumbling tower. My master whispered to me to note how poor the defences were.

The pirates decided to send a letter to Julius Caesar's father. They wanted a ransom of 20 talents of gold, a great weight equal to six grown men. As I knew how to write, they made me pen the letter.

My master was shocked when I told him what the pirates proposed – not shocked at the ransom, but by the paltry sum they demanded.

"Do they set the same price on my life as some low-ranking officer?" he demanded angrily. "Let the ransom be worthy of a nobleman – 50 talents at least!"

So the price was set. The pirate leader sealed the letter with one of my master's rings and sent it off.

The next few weeks passed slowly. My master whiled away the time by writing poetry. He was pleased with his work. One evening he decided to read it to the pirates.

The pirates were eager for any entertainment and listened quietly at first. But soon they began to laugh and jeer at the noble Caesar's work.

My master was furious. He would have slain the pirates on the spot – had his sword not been stolen!

Famous writer
Caesar later became famous for his writing – not for poetry but for his account of how he conquered Gaul (the Roman name for France).

Entertainment
Romans enjoyed chariot races, music and dice games. Some spent hours at the public baths.

The army life
Soldiers, called legionaries, wore armour and carried daggers and swords. After 25 years in the army, they were rewarded with money or land.

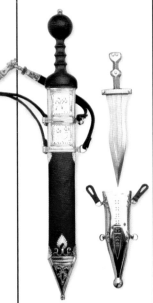

Fortunately, a ship arrived with the ransom and soon afterwards my master and I were set free. I hoped we might go back to Rome, but no. My master had been hatching a plan. We made our way to his friend Flavius, a commander in the Roman army.

Caesar persuaded his friend that the pirates should be stamped out. Flavius gave him a troop of 500 soldiers and a fleet of war galleys.

Within a few days we were in sight of the pirates' island. This time we had the upper hand.

We came ashore while the pirates were asleep. The soldiers, wielding swords and daggers, overran the village and slew most of the gang. The pirate leaders were taken prisoner and brought before Caesar.

My master was in a fine mood and roared that he would set an example to pirates everywhere.

He would show the world that an insult to Rome (though I think he meant an insult to his poetry) would be punished without mercy. Then he gave orders to execute the lot of them.

He vowed no pirate would ever again get away with kidnapping a Roman noble. Indeed, from what I hear, piracy in our time has all but died out. ❖

A slow death
Romans executed criminals in a dreadfully cruel way. They nailed them to wooden crosses and left them to die. This is called crucifixion.

Bottled drink
On long sea journeys pirates preferred to swig bottles of beer – barrels of water soon became too foul to drink.

Wine, women and song
When pirates were ashore they spent a lot of money on drinking and gambling. Silver coins called pieces of eight were the most common money.

Filthy rich!

It was the spring of 1705 and I was sitting on the docks in Bristol, waiting for my uncle. An old sea salt hobbled up and eased himself down beside me. He took a drink from his beer bottle as we watched the boats come and go. Then he began to talk, and strange talk it was too.

"Do you know what it feels like to be filthy rich, boy?" The old sailor leaned his brown, lined face closer to mine. "Can you imagine it?"

"No, sir," I replied truthfully. The greatest wealth I had ever come across was the money to buy new shoes.

"Heavy, that's what! Think what it's like to have piles of gold and silver coins and bags of glittering jewels – more than you or I could ever lift. You can't imagine what a nightmare it is to have more money than you can carry!"

"I'd ask for help, sir," I said.

The old man laughed. "Help? I got more than enough help! When men find out that you're rich they try to rob you left and right."

"I wouldn't mind being rich, sir," I said. "I can say that with honesty."

"Ha! Honesty had nothing to do with it," he spluttered. "Murder and thieving, yes. But if it wasn't for signing on as second mate with old Captain Avery, bless him, I wouldn't have two coins to my name today. You know about Henry Avery the pirate, don't you, boy? He was no common outlaw. Oh no. He was a proper gentleman and the finest leader I ever saw."

Pirate captain
An unpopular captain could be voted out of his job. Normally, he and his crew made decisions together, but during a battle he had total authority.

In the navy
Naval sailors were badly paid and fed. They were flogged with a cat of nine tails for the slightest offence. Many turned to piracy for a better life.

A cat of nine tails was made from nine separate strands of unwound rope.

The sailor to be beaten made his own whip. He finished it off by knotting the ends.

"Way back in 1690, Avery was a captain in the English Royal Navy. He was busy chasing after the French and Spanish. But his mind was ticking over the whole time, saying, 'Henry Avery! There's plunder beyond reckoning out here. And the ocean's a big place. It's big enough for a man to hide safely if he wants to.'

Now Avery wasn't the kind of man to let a good idea sleep. So he left the English Royal Navy and swapped sides to work for the Spanish. He worked as a privateer, a kind of legal pirate, looting enemy ships and sharing the captured treasure with the king of Spain."

"But it didn't take long for Avery to see he was getting nothing from the king in return. So why, he asked himself, should he split the booty? He might as well keep it all for himself.

So Avery became a true-blue pirate and sailed under a pirate flag. He even took the name Long Ben, just so people knew he was no gentleman anymore, but a complete rogue and an out-and-out villain.

Like all things he did, Avery was a big success at pirating. His fame soon spread across land and sea. In ports all over the Atlantic men lined up for the next ship that would take them to him. It wasn't very long before the captain was in command of a proper little fleet of six pirate ships."

Loud hailer
Privateers lived on crowded ships, as extra men were needed to sail any captured vessels. A captain used a speaking trumpet both to talk to his crew and to order the enemy to give up without a fight.

Pirate flag
All pirates had their own flag. Henry Avery's was a version of the Jolly Roger – a skull and crossbones that symbolized death.

Pirate paradise
Madagascar was a lawless land where pirates were said to have several wives at one time.

Cannon balls
These smashed holes in ships. Some cannons could fire cannon balls as as far as 1.5 km (1 mile).

"When I first boarded Captain Avery's ship, the *Fancy*, she was based in Madagascar. I tell you, it's a beautiful tropical island, with just about everything a man could want in life – except for money.

But Avery had good reason for lying here. He was waiting for a treasure fleet. He stationed his ships in a wide arc across the treasure fleet's route, cannons at the ready.

But most of the ships managed to slip past one night. By dawn, only two stragglers were in sight."

"Before long we were within cannon shot of the smaller of the two vessels. We fired and hit her with a lucky shot. We must have frightened the crew out of their wits, for they lowered their sails and surrendered in no time.

We boarded her quickly, smarting at having missed the rest of the fleet. Then the lads who were rummaging in the captain's cabin gave a shout. They'd found great chests stuffed with gold and silver coins. The ship was owned by the Great Mogul, the emperor of India.

We knew he was incredibly wealthy but this was more money than any of us had seen in our lives.

Avery raised his sword and shouted. 'Boys! If this is what the mogul hides on his small ships, what treasure will he have on the big one? Come on! Shall we go after her?'"

Ancient craft
Indian Ocean cargo ships were called dhows. These were first built by Arab shipbuilders who did not use nails. Timbers were held tight with coconut fibre.

Rich rulers
The emperors of India were called Great Moguls. They lived in luxury and built giant palaces, forts and temples.

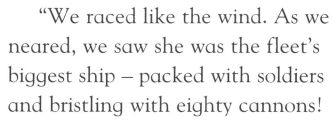

Holy city
The mogul's ships carried Muslims from India on a pilgrimage to Mecca where their prophet, Mohammed, was born. Muslims are expected to visit Mecca at least once in their lives.

"We raced like the wind. As we neared, we saw she was the fleet's biggest ship – packed with soldiers and bristling with eighty cannons!

We fought a furious battle and by the time we boarded our blood was boiling. We found passengers on board – pilgrims on their way home from Arabia. The way we mistreated them would make my hair curl, if I still had any.

But we found such treasure! There was a glittering hoard of coins and jewels beyond compare. Many say it was the biggest booty in the history of pirating. We divided it among us. You might say we all became filthy rich!"

"What about the captain?" I asked.

"He vanished without a trace! That mogul had the English navy scouring the seas for Captain Avery but he was never found. Some folk say he went to Ireland where he lived as a rich and respected gent. Others say he was swindled out of his money and died poor. I doubt we'll ever know," said the old man with a wink. ❖

Splitting the loot
Pirates always divided their treasure into fair shares for all. Sailors got one share, captains one and a half and the commander of the fleet four shares. Those who did not take part in the fighting got less than one share.

21

Dressed to kill
Early buccaneers lived in small groups and dressed in clothes made from animal hides. The clothes stank from the blood of the animals they had slaughtered.

Cattle hunters
These men were the first buccaneers. They got their name from grills, called "boucans", on which they cured beef.

Wild buccaneers

Let me tell you the story of my brilliant career as a buccaneer. My name is John Dunn. I started out, like so many in the Caribbean, living off the land and hunting wild cattle on the island of Hispaniola. We buccaneers were a rough bunch, but we lived by our wits and were free men. That is, until the Spanish killed off the cattle and drove us away. That's when we became pirates.

We attacked Spanish ships until they sailed in fleets we couldn't beat. Then we turned to raiding Spanish towns. And that's when Henry Morgan first crossed my path.

Morgan came to the Caribbean as a young man. He drifted into the same buccaneering life as the rest of us. But while we were happy to plunder tiny villages, Morgan had bigger fish to fry.

One day, in 1688, he dreamed up a mad idea to attack Portobelo – the best-defended town in the Caribbean. And his plan was just fantastic!

Spanish ships
Ships called galleons carried treasures from the Spanish empire in the Americas back to Spain. They sailed in fleets of up to 100 vessels to protect each other against pirate attacks.

Sailors in the crow's nest kept watch for pirates.

A galleon had a large, square sail on each mast.

A crew of about 200 men worked on board.

Cannon

Rudder

Treasure was kept below deck.

The island of Jamaica
England captured this island from Spain in 1655. It was the main base for buccaneer raids on the Spanish, as its governor usually turned a blind eye.

Those of us based in Jamaica jumped at the chance to join the raid. Portobelo was a large and wealthy town, guarded by two great forts that faced out to sea. They were always on alert, so any attacking ship would be blown out of the water as it came in range. Morgan knew this, so he planned to attack from inland.

We came ashore in the dark of night, several miles from Portobelo. As we neared the town we captured a guard and that was it. The way ahead lay wide open.

We swarmed through the streets and attacked both forts. The first gave up to our sword-swinging men. But the second put up a fight that stopped us dead.

Pirate sword
Buccaneers invented a wide-bladed sword called a cutlass. They first used it to butcher cattle.

Morgan called for his men. He had an idea that surprised even the hardest of us.

"We must round up all the monks and nuns in town and use them as shields," he said.

Soon we were forcing our terrified prisoners up scaling ladders.

Morgan gambled that no soldier would shoot them point blank. He was right. Meanwhile our men scrambled up hard behind and poured over the walls.

In no time, the fort was captured and the town was ours! We looted and pillaged. We carried treasure from churches and houses and we found more hidden in gardens and caves. We tortured anyone who refused to hand over money. If that didn't work, we locked them in churches to starve until they changed their minds.

When we finally left Portobelo, we took away 200,000 silver coins and piles of silverware, jewellery and other valuables. It took 150 mules to carry the treasure back to the waiting ship. It was a triumph!

On the rack
Buccaneers stretched their captives on racks to make them reveal where they had hidden their valuables.

Private property
Pirates shared out a ship's cargo. But they were often allowed to keep for themselves the captives' personal items, such as jewellery and pistols.

Once we finished celebrating
our success, Morgan raised a fleet
for his most daring adventure of all.
He planned to attack Panama City.

Again we marched overland to
attack from the back. Day after day
we trekked through hostile jungle.
We were weak with sickness and
hunger when we finally reached
Panama City.

This time we had to beat off
charging horses and stampeding bulls.

But our musket fire cut the enemy down. We took the city by storm.

By this time Morgan was in real trouble. Spain and England had signed a peace treaty and Spain was threatening war again unless Morgan was punished.

So before long Henry Morgan was captured and sent to England to stand trial for piracy. But many English people were pleased Morgan had attacked Spanish towns. So crowds gathered to cheer him on.

Even the king of England fell under his spell. Far from punishing Morgan, the king knighted him and made him governor of Jamaica!

Sir Henry took to his new job with gusto. In a total turnabout, he began to hang pirates, even those who had once sailed with him. He died in peace some years later, which is what I plan to do (but not yet!) now my buccaneer days are over. ❖

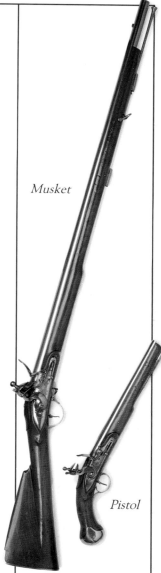

Musket

Pistol

Musket power
Buccaneers were famously good shots. They fought with muskets, which were more accurate than pistols.

Noose

*Wooden
gallows*

Hempen rope

Captain Kidd

Last night I visited my cousin,
William Kidd, who was in jail in
England waiting to be hanged. It had
been years since I last saw him and I
was dismayed by the state he was in.

His words of greeting were curses
and demands for more drink. I could
see he had not come to terms with
going to the gallows the next day.

"None of this would have
happened if I hadn't been set up,"
he explained. "I could have made a
fortune, I tell you. I had permission
to raid French ships from the king of
England himself.

Yet it all began to go wrong
with the *Adventure Galley*.
What a wormy old tub!
She wasn't much of a ship and
my second mate did me no
favours with the crew he found
in New York. They were the
worst ruffians in town."

"The bad tempers and plotting began at once," he told me.

"Gunner Moore was the worst – a nasty bully who was ready to fight at the drop of a hat. The day he grabbed a chisel and came at me was too much. It was him or me. So I hit him hard with a wooden bucket and he fell heavily on the deck. Bad luck that he died, but the scoundrel had it coming!"

Pirate's licence
An official licence to raid ships of an enemy country was formally set out in "letters of marque".

Hard justice
Discipline was harsh on all ships. If a crewman was murdered on a pirate ship, the killer could be tied to his victim and thrown overboard. For lesser crimes, a pirate was marooned – left on a desert island to starve.

I asked why he hadn't gone straight back to port.

"Listen, I had rich and powerful men backing the voyage," he said. "Lord Bellamont was among them and he would have been furious if I'd come back empty-handed.

So I pressed onwards. We had a few successes along the way. We seized two French ships and took a pretty pile of gold and precious gems from them."

I knew people were saying that they weren't French ships at all. But in the circumstances I said nothing. It was kinder to stay silent.

"That's when it all went wrong." He grimaced as he spoke. "It had taken far too long to find treasure and the poor food supplies had made some of the crew as sick as dogs. They were all in a foul mood and demanded a share-out of the treasure – then and there."

"They were so menacing I feared they would mutiny and take my ship. So I agreed rather than wait until we came to port, as was customary.

I was in real trouble now. Dividing the loot with the crew meant the share for my backers had been grabbed by the men. That would be hard to explain.

As soon as I could, I got rid of the worst of my crew by leaving them on shore. Then I started to navigate homeward. Just in case, I stopped off and buried the remaining treasure. I hid some on Hispaniola and some on Gardiner's Island near New York."

Which way? Pirates used a compass to help them find their way across the oceans. The needle of a compass always points north.

Handcuffs

19th-century ankle fetters

Chains
These were locked on to prisoners' wrists and ankles to prevent them from escaping. In Boston, Kidd was put in handcuffs weighing 7 kg (16 lbs).

I asked William what had happened when he got back.

"I heard that my backers, especially Lord Bellamont, were spreading vile rumours about me. I was accused of being a common pirate and of murdering my crew. As a result I was arrested when I landed at Boston.

None of the charges against me was fair. I was sure I could prove I had done nothing wrong. But the power and influence of Lord Bellamont and his friends were such that I was clapped in irons and sent back to England, where they flung me into this filthy hole of a prison.

When I finally met Lord Bellamont, he refused my offer of the Hispaniola treasure for my freedom. Later, I learned he sent a ship to search for it, although it returned with nothing."

Life in jail
Prisoners were locked up in dark, cold cells. They had to buy their own food and clothes. If they had no money they starved.

Rats
Conditions in prisons were foul and overcrowded. As well as sharing cells with fellow prisoners, captives had to live with lice, fleas and rats.

"I'll never forgive Lord Bellamont and his fine friends for what they've done to me."

Then William pressed a crumpled piece of paper into my hand. "Here, cousin," he said, "I want you to give this to my poor wife."

High court
The House of Commons was one of the highest courts in the land. It was, and still is, a meeting place for members of parliament in Britain.

Proof of innocence
Documents that went missing before Kidd's trial could have helped prove his innocence. One hundred years later they were found in a government desk drawer.

I pushed the note into my pocket as William started rambling on about the trial.

"I was taken to court on the grand charges of piracy and murder. But I was not allowed to have a lawyer to defend me.

I tried to show that I was innocent and I told what happened on the voyage as best I could. Then two members of my crew came forward to confirm my tale. But they turned on me and supported all my accusers' lies. I believe they must have been offered free pardons to blacken my name.

That sealed my fate and I was sentenced to hang. Will you be there tomorrow and say a prayer for my soul?" my poor cousin asked bitterly.

I promised I would.

So the next day I joined the rabble waiting by the River Thames to see the hanging. I saw William dragged to the gallows. He was too drunk to stand. The hangman had to hold him up to put the noose around his neck.

At the first try, the rope snapped and William fell on the riverbank. He had to be picked up and hanged again. Later his body was put on display.

As I left the sorry scene, I recalled the note he had given me. I unfolded what looked like a map. It could have been Hispaniola or Gardiner's Island, or somewhere else entirely.

As I studied it, a sudden wind tore the map from my grasp. All I could do was watch it swirl away, lost forever.

A worse death
"Robbery on the high seas" carried a death penalty all over the world.
A few authorities favoured roasting pirates alive over hot coals.

A warning
After a pirate had been hanged, the dead body was cut down from the gallows and put inside the metal hoops of a gibbet. The body, which hung there slowly rotting, was a grisly warning of the fate that awaits all pirates.

Treasure island
Oak Island's money pit was built from a natural shaft. Several people have lost their lives trying to find out what is hidden there.

A meter gives information about a find.

The detector head picks up the magnetic field given off by metal.

Modern tool
Today's hunters use metal detectors which they sweep over the ground. A loud buzz tells the hunter where metal is hidden.

Treasure Island

Did Captain Kidd find a quiet island and bury treasure there? To this day, we don't know.

What is true is that in 1795, nearly one hundred years after Kidd's death, a young boy was digging on Oak Island off Canada. He stumbled on a deep shaft that became known as the "Money Pit of Oak Island".

Many believed buried treasure was hidden at the bottom. Old folk tales told of pirate ships and strange flashing lights. What the first diggers found was a fiendish trap 50 metres deep, with log platforms blocking the shaft at 3-metre intervals.

When the treasure hunters hit the 30-metre level, they found a carved stone etched with strange markings. Digging deeper, they set off a booby trap. As a pocket of trapped air escaped, gallons of salt water poured in by a side tunnel.

It completely flooded the shaft and made it impossible to go on.

Then in the 1970s, a team with underwater cameras tried to explore the pit. Probing the dark water, the team found wooden chests and a severed human hand floating in the gloom.

Several divers went down to explore but the shaft walls were so weak they kept collapsing. The men were forced to abandon the hunt for Captain Kidd's treasure. For all we know, it may be there to this day. ❖

Mad, bad Blackbeard

My worst job ever was to hunt down a pirate named Blackbeard. He was as mad as he was bad. His evil ways filled people with fear all along the coast of Virginia and the Carolinas. Believe me, I was not happy when the governor of Virginia said, "Maynard. I want you to take a ship and hunt that dog, Blackbeard!"

Blackbeard was cruel and strong and had a murderous temper. He was all but impossible when he drank rum, which he did often. Then he would slip into terrifying moods.

One time, he locked himself and several men below deck. Then he lit cannon fuses that filled the air with choking fumes. His terrified men begged for mercy, then collapsed before he let them out. Blackbeard didn't let them forget who had held out the longest.

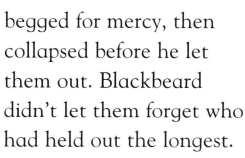

Blackbeard's flag
The skeleton has a spear and hourglass. The hourglass shows time running out – a ship should surrender immediately or no one would be spared.

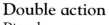

Double action
Pistols were slow to reload so pirates carried several. They fired a pistol once, then used it as a handy club.

My crew knew of Blackbeard's reputation too.

We had all heard that this pirate was in a class of his own. He had a taste for terror that he used so well that people lost the will to resist. They simply surrendered when they caught sight of him.

Blackbeard knew he could horrify his victims with nothing more than his outlandish ways. That was why he flew an especially grim pirate flag from the mast of his ship.

Blackbeard dressed like a crazy man too. He lived at a time when hardly anybody had a beard, but he grew a long, shaggy black bush that he braided and tied up with ribbons. This was the source of his pirate name.

When Blackbeard waded into a fight, he wore a shoulder sling with several pistols hanging from it.

He also carried daggers and a razor-sharp cutlass that he slashed through the air in a most terrifying manner. He liked to boast he was as heavily armed as ten men.

Blackbeard's finishing touch was to poke two smouldering fuses under the brim of his hat. These wreathed his face with thick, grey smoke and gave him a devilish appearance. At the same time he shouted and cursed. The effect was dreadful – many threw down their weapons without trying to fight.

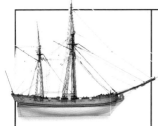

Speedy sailing
Fast sailing ships of the time were called sloops. They had shallow hulls and could sail close to shore. Pirates used sloops to hide out in bays, then pounce on their victims.

Early grenades
At that time, they were bottles filled with gunpowder and bits of metal. They made lots of noise as they exploded but usually didn't do much harm.

Blackbeard made raids up and down the coast, taking a huge toll of ships and terrifying small towns. Then, in November 1718, I set off in a fast ship to track him down.

It took a few days of hunting before I found him in the small inlet where he liked to hide. He often went there to scrape off barnacles that grew on the ship's hull and slowed it down in the water.

When the pirates saw my ship approach they fired their cannons. They were good shots and wounded over a dozen of my sailors.

They took to the sea and
I could see we were in for a
dreadful fight. However, we
held fire as I wanted to lure
the pirates on to my ship.

As our ships drew close
the pirates flung grenades at us.
Then they charged. They leaped
over the rails of their ship,
waving knives and axes.

It was exactly the reckless
move I was counting on.
Most of my men were armed
and hidden below deck.
At my signal, they attacked.

Giant man

In Blackbeard's time, around three hundred years ago, the average man was a lot smaller. So at 1.9 m (6 feet 4 inches) and 113 kg (250 pounds), Blackbeard towered over most people.

The sailors rushed at the pirates and brutal hand-to-hand fighting broke out. In the chaos I found myself facing Blackbeard. He really was a giant! We fired our pistols, but missed each other.

We both drew our swords. The great pirate landed a terrific blow that snapped my blade clean in two.

Preparing for battle

Blackbeard fortified himself for battle by mixing together gunpowder and strong rum. Then he gulped it down and attacked!

For an instant I thought I was a goner. He came at me again. Then a sailor stepped in and stopped him in his tracks with a sword blow to the face. This gave me time to draw my second pistol and fire a ball into him point-blank.

Blackbeard swayed but stayed on his feet. From somewhere I found a third pistol and fired another shot into him just as one of my boys swung a sword at his neck. He went down at last and lay dead on the deck.

This was the signal to the rest of his crew to leap overboard and swim for freedom. In a mad moment of triumph (that I'm not proud of) I cut off Blackbeard's head and tied it to the bow of our ship. Then we sailed home to collect our reward for putting an end to his pirate career. ❖

Faulty aim
Pistols fired shot as big as marbles. But pirates still had to fire them at point-blank range to hit anything.

Early end
Most pirates only had short lives. However, many more died from fighting, disease and shipwrecks than were ever caught and hanged.

Glossary

Amphorae
Heavy clay jars used by the ancient Romans to store wine and oil.

Buccaneers
Caribbean pirates of the late 1600s who raided Spanish ships and towns. The name comes from settlers on the island of Hispaniola, who smoked cattle meat on grills called "boucans".

Cannon fuses
Smouldering lengths of twisted cord that were used to light cannons.

Cat of nine tails
A whip with nine long braids that was used to punish sailors. The whip left a man's back raw and bleeding.

Cutlass
A wide-bladed sword first used as a weapon by buccaneers.

Flagship
A fleet's most important ship; it carried the commander and his flag.

Gallows
A wooden platform and frame from which hung a noose. People were taken here to be hanged.

Gibbet
A wooden hoist with a set of chains and metal hoops used to hang a dead body for all to see.

Governors
In the 1600s and 1700s, America was a collection of colonies ruled by governors sent out from England, France or Spain. A governor ruled with all the authority of the king or queen back home.

Grenade
The grenades used by pirates were bottles filled with gunpowder and pieces of metal, which exploded with a bang.

Jolly Roger
The black flag flown by pirates. Different pirates had different designs. The most famous version was a white skull and crossbones.

Letters of marque
An official document giving a ship's captain permission to rob or capture ships of an enemy country.

Musket
A long-barrelled gun that fired a round ball. A musket was so accurate that a buccaneer could shoot a hole right through the middle of a coin.

Navigate
To get from place to place and to stay on course. Pirates used compasses, charts and measurements of the sun to navigate.

Pieces of eight
Spanish silver coins were called pieces of eight because they were often cut into eight pie-shaped slices, called bits. A two-bit slice, or quarter, was the most common piece.

Privateer
A captain with official permission to attack and rob enemy ships. In return, the king or queen got a share of the loot.

Rhodes
A big island off the coast of Turkey. In Roman times it was the home of many poets, artists and thinkers.

Roman army
Ancient Rome had a huge army of 300,000 men to keep law and order in the empire.

Roman empire
The Roman empire lasted hundreds of years. At its height, it sprawled from Britain to Syria and the Middle East.

Royal Navy
The rulers of England built a strong navy to protect the country from invasion and to guard overseas colonies.

Talent
A talent was a measure of money in Greek and Roman times. One talent of gold weighed 26 kg (58 lbs).